Giraffes

Giraffes

by Sarah Albee

Reader's Digest

Published by The Reader's Digest Association Limited

London • New York • Sydney • Montreal

CONTENTS

Chapter 1

A giraffe story

Day care

For the first four or five months of their lives, baby giraffes rest and play in small groups called crèches while their mothers search for food.

The sun is shining across the African savannah for the rainy season has finally ended. A giraffe is ready to have her baby. With a thud, a bundle falls nearly 2 metres to the ground. Little Giraffe is born. The newborn calf is unhurt, and her mother nuzzles her lovingly.

About 20 minutes later, Little Giraffe staggers to her feet. She wobbles a bit on her long, thin legs but soon gets steadier. Already, she's as tall as an adult man. Two little horns, now flat against her head, will pop up in a week or so. For two weeks, Mother Giraffe hides her baby in tall grass to keep her safe from lions and hyenas.

Little Giraffe spends most of the time lying down but, as her legs grow stronger, she will begin to walk more and more. When she is hungry, she bleats and mews for her mother, who never wanders too far away.

Several months go by, and Little Giraffe grows quickly. She still drinks milk from her mother, but now she joins the group of other giraffes as they look for tasty acacia leaves. She plays with her cousins and other young giraffe friends under the watchful eyes of an adult female giraffe while the rest of their mothers go off in search of food.

One day, while Little Giraffe's mother is guarding the crèche, she sounds an alarm call. With snorts and hisses, she alerts the other adults grazing nearby to come quickly. Standing nearly 5 metres above the ground, she has a great view of the plain. With her sharp eyes, Mother Giraffe has spotted a female lion creeping slowly towards the group of young giraffes. The other mothers run quickly back to the crèche. Little Giraffe races to her mother, who positions herself above her to protect her baby.

The lion stops, stands up and tosses her head. She knows very well that one swift kick from Mother Giraffe's front legs could be deadly. The lion gives up the hunt and trots away.

Giant giraffes

Giraffes' ancestors, which lived around 25 million years ago may have been even taller than giraffes are today.

DID YOU KNOW?

Some scientists believe that other kinds of animals, such as zebras and antelopes, deliberately graze near groups of giraffes. The giraffes' ability to spot danger from a distance helps to protect these other animals, too.

Giraffes burp a lot – to let out the gas created in their stomachs as they try to digest all the leaves they eat.

Five years go by, and Little Giraffe is now fully grown. She walks over the savannah with a group of other giraffes, munching leaves high above the ground and calling to the other giraffes from great distances to let them know where she is. She knows her friends and relatives by the markings on their coats, as each one is a bit different from another. She has also made friends with a little oxpecker bird, who loves to perch on her back and pluck annoying insects from her furry coat.

Little Giraffe will soon be ready to have a calf of her own. She will stay in the same area where her mother lives for the rest of her life.

It's a stretch

Male and female giraffes eat leaves that grow at different heights. Males reach up to leaves growing higher than they are, with their heads and necks stretched fully upwards. Females eat at the same level as their body, sometimes with their head and neck slightly bent.

Chapter 2

The body of a giraffe

The neck of a fully grown
giraffe is around 2 metres
long – taller than most
adult humans.

Tall and towering

Giraffes are the tallest animals in the world. Males are more than 5 metres high, females are nearly 5 metres. Their height comes from their long legs and long neck.

Being the tallest animal helps giraffes to survive, because they can reach food that other animals cannot and so they do not have to compete with other animals for food. Their height also allows them to spot predators (animals that might attack and eat them) when they are far away, giving the giraffes time to seek safety.

Giraffes have a brown mane, which is short and bristly running the length of their necks. They also have long tails with a tuft of long, stiff hair at the ends – perfect for swatting away insects.

At first glance, giraffes may look similar, but their coats vary quite a lot. The background colour ranges from white to tan to yellowish, their spots may be anything from light orange to dark brown, and the shape of the spots differs. One type of giraffe has large rectangular patches; others have irregular blotches. Although the pattern on a giraffe's coat remains the same throughout its life, its colour darkens as the giraffe grows older.

Long legs

With its super-long legs, a giraffe can cover quite a lot of ground, even when it is just walking. You would have to run to keep up with it.

A giraffe has two strides – walking and galloping. When walking, the giraffe swings both right legs forward at the same time and then both left legs. Only one other four-legged animal walks this way – the camel. Other animals with four legs, such as dogs, walk by moving diagonally opposite legs – the front right and back left legs and then the front left and back right ones.

As it gallops, the giraffe swings its great neck backwards and forwards like a huge rocking horse. At a gallop, a giraffe moves 3 metres with each stride, thundering along at more than 30 miles per hour. Most of the time, though, giraffes stroll slowly, munching leaves as they go.

Giraffes have cloven feet, which means that their feet are divided in two. Their feet are covered with tough hoofs. Their hoofprints are about 30 centimetres long.

DID YOU KNOW?

With their long legs, giraffes can easily jump over things that are the height of a tall man.

A giraffe's front legs are longer than the back ones, so its body has a slightly downward slope.

Horn of plenty

All giraffes are born with horns on top of their heads. Some male giraffes have as many as five. As the giraffe gets older, its horns gradually grow harder and stiffer.

Giraffes have great hearing. Their pointed ears are 20 centimetres long and can swivel in several directions.

Sight and smell

With their height and excellent eyesight, giraffes can see for miles across the flat African plains. Their huge brown eyes are protected by long lashes and are set on the sides of their heads so that the animal can see all around. Some animals feel safer near giraffes because the giraffes can detect enemies when they are still far away. Some scientists believe that giraffes see colours quite well.

But, unlike us, giraffes don't have tear ducts, which water to clean dirt away from our eyes. So they use their long tongue to clean their eyes, instead.

Giraffes have a good sense of smell. A mother giraffe quickly learns to recognise her baby by the way it smells. Giraffe scent glands give off an odour that enables them to recognise one another. Their odour probably also protects them from certain annoying insects.

DID YOU KNOW?

Many people think that giraffes are silent animals, but they are not. Although they tend to be quiet, giraffes can make a variety of sounds, such as moans, alarm calls, snorts, hisses and flute-like notes. Baby giraffes bleat and mew. Mother giraffes, calling to their babies, may even bellow.

Snatching some sleep

Giraffes rest after dark in an open area where they can keep a watchful eye out for danger. They lie down for a few hours to rest and digest their food, catching bits of sleep here and there. Giraffes usually sleep deeply for only 1 to 12 minutes at a time and for a total of only about 20 minutes a night. They may keep each eye open alternately to be on the alert for predators. When they do lie down and sleep, they bend their neck backwards to rest on their back leg, like a handle.

Keeping clean

Giraffes groom themselves by biting and licking. Having a 2 metre long neck and a tongue that is 45 centimetres long helps them to reach most parts of their bodies.

Giraffes also have cleaning helpers – birds that live with them. The buffalo weaver and oxpecker birds perch on the giraffes and pluck out biting insects from their fur. The birds also help by calling shrilly when they spot danger.

Giraffes sometimes
take a nap standing up.

A dozing pose

Giraffes sometimes sleep in a sitting position, with their legs folded beneath them, but with their neck held upright.

Lunch munchers

Giraffes spend half of each day eating, usually in the hours before sunrise and after sunset.

Plant eaters

Giraffes are herbivores, which means they eat only plants. Acacia tree leaves are their favourite. Most acacia trees have sharp thorns, sometimes 5 centimetres long. But these don't bother the giraffes. With their strong, flexible lips and long, sticky tongues, the giraffes gather the leaves into their mouths and tear them off the branches by pulling their heads away.

Luckily for acacia trees, giraffes do not devour all the leaves on a tree before moving on. One reason may be the stinging ants that live in hollow areas of the acacia tree branches. They protect the tree by swarming onto the giraffes' faces and necks. The giraffes tolerate the stings for a short time but usually move on to the next tree.

Chewing their cud

Just like cows, giraffes belong to a type of animal called 'ruminants'. Ruminants have a stomach with four compartments that help to break down the tough leaves that the animals eat.

When giraffes are not eating, they are chewing their cud, which is a ball of partly digested leaves that travels back up their throat into their mouths so they can grind it down even more.

Drinking – a tall order

For the world's tallest animals, drinking water is a challenging task because it is difficult for them to reach the level of the water.

A giraffe's front legs are so long that the giraffe must spread them far to the sides in order to lower its head to the water. This is a rather awkward position. Sometimes giraffes kneel down to drink, but this is also a difficult position to get into and out of, too.

Have you ever bent your head down very low (or stood on your head) and then straightened up quickly? If you have, you may have felt slightly dizzy. Imagine, then, how a giraffe feels when it lowers its head 5 metres. Fortunately, a giraffe has a special system to manage this problem. Inside the giraffe's neck are blood vessels that stretch and valves (like little trap doors) inside the blood vessels that prevent all the blood from rushing to the animal's head as it dips way below the level of its heart. Without these valves, the giraffe could faint every time it drinks because of the rapid changes in its blood pressure.

After a giraffe stands upright, it usually stretches its neck and back legs to get the blood flowing freely again.

DID YOU KNOW?

Like camels, giraffes can go for weeks without drinking any water. They get most of the moisture they need from the leaves they eat.

When a giraffe's legs are splayed, the giraffe is vulnerable to attack because it can't quickly stand up to flee or defend itself.

Chapter 4

Surviving in the wild

A mother giraffe usually
returns to the same place
every time she has a baby.

Young giraffes

After carrying the baby inside her body for about 14 months, a mother giraffe gives birth standing up, usually to a single calf.

A giraffe is huge from the moment it is born. A newborn calf is nearly 2 metres tall and weighs 75 kilograms – the size of an adult human. Then it grows about 8 centimetres a month until it is full size – around 5 metres tall and weighing a tonne. That's 1,000 kilograms!

Young calves are playful and love to run around together. For the first four to five months of their lives, the calves stay together in a small nursery group called a crèche. They play or rest while their mothers search for food. At least one adult female stays with the calves for protection. Young giraffes are most often attacked by predators during their first year of life. Once they are a year old, though, they have a very good chance of living to 20 to 25 years of age.

Giraffe herds

Giraffes live in loose, open groups, often called herds, that may spread across half a mile of the savannah.

A giraffe herd may consist of mothers and their young, or be all males, or be a mix of males and females. The members of giraffe herds are constantly changing. The herds tend not to have a leader.

Most herds have up to 20 giraffes, but because of the giraffes' large size, the adult giraffes do not have to live closely together for protection. With their extreme height and excellent eyesight, they are able to warn the others in the herd of any danger.

Giraffes' territories can vary greatly, anywhere from 5 square kilometres to 600 square kilometres, but average about 150 square kilometres – about as big as a medium-sized city. Males eventually leave their home territory to mate, but females tend to stay close to the area where they were born for life.

Living in small groups
helps giraffes to protect
themselves and their young.

Giraffes often position themselves so that they can look out for enemies approaching from any direction.

Protecting themselves

Adult giraffes have few enemies. That's because they are so big and because the special markings on their coat help them to blend in with their surroundings.

The only predators that adult giraffes fear, besides man, are lions and crocodiles. Adult giraffes are most in danger when they bend down to drink or lie down to sleep. Fortunately for giraffes, they don't need to drink very often and they sleep for only a few minutes at a time – sometimes standing up.

Young giraffes, though, are often attacked by lions, leopards, hyenas and wild dogs. Mother giraffes protect their calves by kicking attackers with their powerful front legs, which are capable of killing a full-grown lion.

Chapter 5

Giraffes in the world

Leaf spots

Giraffes with dark brown, leaf-shaped spots on a yellowish background are called Masai giraffes.

Giraffes with large patches that are clearly outlined are called reticulated giraffes.

Spot the spots

Although each individual giraffe has its own special colour and spot pattern on its coat, scientists have identified and named roughly eight groups of giraffes that have similar patterns and share the same home territory.

Some groups of giraffes have large spots, others have small ones. Certain giraffes have round spots, others have spots with sides. Spots can also be star-shaped, leaf-shaped or irregularly shaped.

Only relative

The giraffe has only one close relative, the okapi. Although the okapi has a dark coat (with no patches) and stripes on its legs, it has an elongated neck. The okapi lives in the African rain forests.

Where giraffes live

Although 25 million years ago, giraffes lived in what is now Africa, Europe and Asia, today's giraffes are found only in Africa, south of the Sahara Desert. Giraffes live on the savannah and in open woodlands, most often where acacia trees grow. Once hunted by humans for food, their hides and the hair on their tails, giraffes are now protected by law in many countries.

The word giraffe comes from an old Arab word meaning 'one who walks swiftly'.

FAST FACTS ABOUT GIRAFFES

SCIENTIFIC NAME	*Giraffa camelopardalis*
CLASS	Mammals
FAMILY	*Giraffidae*
SIZE	Males 5.4 metres tall Females 4.8 metres tall
WEIGHT	Males between 900 and 1,800 kilograms Females between 750 and 1,300 kilograms
HABITAT	Savannahs and open woodlands with tall trees
SPEED	Up to 30 miles per hour

GLOSSARY OF **wild** WORDS

acacia	a tree that grows in warm areas and has feather-like leaves	ducts	passages or tubes in which liquid or air flows
blood vessels	the arteries and veins in a body through which blood flows to and from the heart	groom	to clean fur, skin, or feathers by an animal
calf	a baby or young giraffe	habitat	the natural environment where an animal or plant lives
cloven	describes a hoof, divided in two	herbivore	an animal that eats only plants
cud	food that comes back into an animal's mouth from the stomach for the animal to chew again	mammal	an animal with a backbone and hair on its body that drinks milk from its mother when it is born

44

mane	hair on the head or neck of an animal		savannah	a flat grassland area with scattered trees in a hot region of the world
predator	an animal that hunts and eats other animals to survive		species	a group of plants or animals that are the same in many ways
prey	animals that are hunted by other animals for food		splay	to spread outward in an awkward way
ruminants	hoofed mammals that have four chambers in their stomachs and that chew cud		swivel	to twist or turn around on the same spot
			valve	a device that starts or stops the flow of liquid

INDEX

CREDITS

Front Cover: Getty Images Ltd/PhotoDisc; 1-3 Brand X Pictures; 4-7 IT Stock;
8 Getty Images Ltd/Digital Vision; 8 L Nova Development Corporation;
10 Brand X Pictures; 10-13 Getty Images Ltd/Digital Vision;
13 Nova Development Corporation; 14-16 Getty Images Ltd/Digital Vision;
18-19 Corbis; 19 ImageState/John Foxx Images; 20 Corbis;
22 Nova Development Corporation; 23 Dynamic Graphics, Inc.;
23 R Photolibrary.com/PhotoDisc; 24-29 Getty Images Ltd/Digital Vision;
30-31 Corbis; 32-35 Getty Images Ltd/PhotoDisc; 36 Image 100;
40-41 Getty Images Ltd/PhotoDisc; 42-43 Dynamic Graphics, Inc.;
44-45 Getty Images Ltd/PhotoDisc; 47-48 Getty Images Ltd/Digital Vision;
Back Cover: Getty Images Ltd/Digital Vision

Giraffes is an *All About Animals* fact book
published by The Reader's Digest Association, Inc.

Written by Sarah Albee

Copyright © 2005 The Reader's Digest Association, Inc.
This edition was adapted and published in 2008 by
The Reader's Digest Association Limited
11 Westferry Circus, Canary Wharf, London E14 4HE
Reprinted in 2010

Editor: Rachel Warren Chadd
Designer: Nicola Liddiard
Art editor: Simon Webb

® Reader's Digest is a registered trademark of
The Reader's Digest Association, Inc.

We are committed both to the quality of our products and the service we provide
to our customers. We value your comments, so please do contact us on
08705 113366 or via our website at www.readersdigest.co.uk

If you have any comments or suggestions about the content of our books,
email us at gbeditorial@readersdigest.co.uk

Printed in China

ISBN: 978 0 276 44322 0
Book code: 640-005 UP0000-2
Oracle code: 504500064H.00.24